WORLD SOCCER LEGENDS

MEGAN RAPINOE

Abbeville Press Publishers

New York · London

A portion of this book's proceeds are donated to the **Hugo Bustamante AYSO Playership Fund**, a national scholarship program to help ensure that no child misses the chance to play AYSO Soccer. Donations to the fund cover the cost of registration and a uniform for a child in need.

Statistics are current as of January 2020.

Text by Illugi Jökulsson
Design and layout: Árni Torfason

For the English-language edition
Project Editors: David Fabricant and Lauren Bucca
Copyediting: Ashley Benning
Layout: Ada Rodriguez
Production manager: Louise Kurtz

PHOTOGRAPHY CREDITS

Getty Images: front cover (Otto Greule Jr/Stringerp), 11 (Bob Thomas/Popperfoto), p. 14 (Catherine Steenkeste), p. 17 (Jed Jacobsohn/Allsport), p. 19 (Darren Abate), p. 21 (Beck Starr/WireImage), p. 23 (Stanley Chou), p. 24 (Lars Baron–FIFA), p. 27 (Lars Baron–FIFA), pp. 30–31 (Charlotte Wilson/Offside), p. 34 (Eric Verhoeven/Soccrates), p. 35 and back cover bottom (Marcio Machado), p. 41 (Alex Grimm), p. 43 (Simon Bruty/Sports Illustrated), p. 44 (Marc Atkins), p. 56 (Emilio Andreoli), p. 57 (Emilio Andreoli), p. 59 top left (Randy Holmes), p. 59 bottom left (Theo Wargo)

Shutterstock: pp. 2–3 (twobee), pp. 6–7 and back cover top (Jose Breton-Pics Action), pp. 8–9 (Maddy M), p. 13 (Romain Biard), p. 32 (feelphoto), p. 33 (feelphoto), p. 37 (Jose Breton-Pics Action), p. 38 top (Frederic Legrand), p. 38 bottom (lev radin), p. 39 (lev radin), p. 45 (Jose Breton-Pics Action), pp. 46–47 (Jose Breton-Pics Action), p. 48 top (Romain Biard), p. 48 bottom (feelphoto), p. 49 top (feelphoto), p. 49 middle (Jose Breton-Pics Action), p. 49 bottom (Jose Breton-Pics Action), p. 50 top (feelphoto), p. 50 middle (Jose Breton-Pics Action), p. 50 bottom (feelphoto), p. 51 top (feelphoto), p. 51 bottom (Jose Breton-Pics Action), p. 52 and back cover middle (feelphoto), p. 53 Krieger (Romain Biard), p. 53 Horan (Jose Breton-Pics Action), p. 53 Lloyd (Romain Biard), p. 53 Press (Romain Biard), p. 53 Pugh (Leonard Zhukovsky), p. 53 Ellis (Jose Breton-Pics Action), p. 54 top (JStone), pp. 54–55 bottom (Word City Studio), p. 59 right (Debby Wong), pp. 60–61 (Jose Breton-Pics Action)

Wikimedia Commons: pp. 10–11 (Fogbank, CC BY-SA 3.0), p. 16 (H. M. Paget), pp. 28–29 (The White House), pp. 62–63 (Romain Biard)

First edition
10 9 8 7 6 5 4 3 2 1

Library of Congress Cataloging-in-Publication Data

Names: Illugi Jökulsson, author.
Title: Megan Rapinoe / Illugi Jökulsson.
Description: First edition. | New York : Abbeville Press Publishers, 2020.
| Series: World soccer legends | Audience: Ages 7-13 | Audience: Grades
2-3 | Summary: "Traces Megan Rapinoe's rise to stardom, from her
childhood in a soccer crazy Northern California family, to her
outstanding college career at the University of Portland, to her
co-captaincy of the dominant U.S. women's team"— Provided by publisher.

Identifiers: LCCN 2020003227 | ISBN 9780789213686 (hardcover)
Subjects: LCSH: Rapinoe, Megan,—Juvenile literature. | Women soccer
players—United States—Biography—Juvenile literature. | Soccer
players—United States—Biography—Juvenile literature.
Classification: LCC GV942.7.R366 I45 2020 | DDC 796.334092 [B]--dc23
LC record available at https://lccn.loc.gov/2020003227

For bulk and premium sales and for text adoption procedures, write to Customer Service Manager, Abbeville Press, 655 Third Avenue, New York, NY 10017, or call 1-800-ARTBOOK.

Visit Abbeville Press online at www.abbeville.com.

CONTENTS

THE STAR OF 2019

In the summer of 2019, the US women's national soccer team won their second World Cup in a row. The team steamrolled most of their opponents in the tournament. Despite the US squad's insistence that the most important ingredients in their victory were teamwork and solidarity, there is no question that the brightest star of the team, and of the tournament as a whole, was Megan Rapinoe. With her determination, cheerfulness, unique focus, and fighting spirit, both on and off the field, Rapinoe's light shone brilliantly that summer. She would have stood out even if she hadn't dyed her hair pink. Though there are many aspects of Megan Rapinoe's career worth mentioning—not least her verbal sparring with the president of the United States—her achievement on the field matters the most.

Mount Shasta
and Heart Lake

HER HOMETOWN

Megan Rapinoe was born and raised in Redding, California, which sits at the northernmost tip of the Sacramento Valley, in the heart of Redwood Country. The city is practically nestled at the base of the 14,180-foot Mount Shasta on the southern end of the Cascade Range.

In the beginning of the nineteenth century, this region was home to the indigenous Wintu. When European explorers and settlers arrived and began building their homes there, they brought with them infectious diseases the indigenous population had no resistance to, and most of the Wintu eventually died. In 1844, Pierson B. Reading established the first European settlement in the area, which went by the name of Poverty Flats for a time. More and more outsiders arrived during the Gold Rush that began in 1848, but it was not until the Central Pacific Railroad built a terminus in the area that a proper town grew. The name Redding was chosen in 1872 to honor businessman and politician Benjamin B. Redding, who was working as a land agent for the railroad and had also served as mayor of Sacramento.

The town has grown steadily ever since. Its economy relied heavily on the mining industry in the early twentieth century, and in the 1950s logging also became important. Construction of Shasta Dam roughly ten miles from Redding in the Cascade Mountains began in 1938. The energy produced by the dam then boosted the town even further. The population stands now at about 90,000.

As in many other small US cities, the residents of Redding are conservative, both socially and politically. Megan Rapinoe ruffled many feathers when she began to openly advocate for liberal values, call out racist sentiments, and champion LGBTQ rights. Rapinoe has also openly criticized Redding's admiration of Fox News and Donald Trump. Nevertheless, when push comes to shove, Rapinoe remains loyal to her hometown, and the residents of Redding stand by their local girl's side.

"I feel like Redding is kind of this underdog, hardworking, blue-collar, is-what-it-is kind of town, and I try to take that with me," Rapinoe told ESPN.

HER FAMILY

Megan Rapinoe comes from a family of seven. Her father Jim runs a construction company, while her mother Denise is a waitress at a popular restaurant in Redding. Megan and her fraternal twin Rachael are the youngest of the siblings, with five years between them and their older brother Brian.

When Megan was still very young, the Rapinoes moved from central Redding to Palo Cedro, about eight miles away. The family's new home was close to their church but also very near the countryside. It was a wonderful place to grow up, and the energetic young Rapinoe was never idle. Their mother recalled for ESPN how Brian taught his younger sisters how to catch crawfish in the creek and gave them lessons in soccer moves in their side yard. "It wasn't like he drilled them. He let them do it their own way," said their mother. "It was just the cutest thing, and we remember it so clearly."

Muffin and Ma Barker

Twins Rachael and Megan were always up to something, but at heart the sisters were totally different. Their grandfather captured the distinction in the nicknames he gave them, as Rapinoe recalled in the *Players' Tribune* in June 2019. Rachael was Muffin, and Megan was Ma Barker, the notorious 1920s gangster. "That sort of paints the picture for you," Megan said. "I had a lot of energy, to put it mildly."

As the two entered adolescence, Rapinoe found it increasingly difficult to identify with the role she felt society had prescribed for women. As usual, she sought consolation and support from her sister. "I used to follow Rachael around. . . . I was always right on her heels, about two feet behind her, for the entirety of seventh grade. . . . She just had it all figured out. So I was her shadow, and I was totally cool with that."

Megan Rapinoe hugs her mother Denise after the 2019 Women's World Cup final in Lyon, France, on July 7, 2019.

SUPPORTING HER BIG BROTHER

One of the most dramatic and challenging chapters of Megan Rapinoe's life revolved around her older brother Brian. At five years their senior, he was a role model to Megan and her twin sister Rachael as they were growing up. He was a lighthearted and charming jokester and impossible not to like. He was always supportive and protective of his little sisters, and the girls adored him unconditionally. When Megan was in second grade, she once strode into the classroom from the playground, stood with her arms akimbo, and boldly declared: "Brian Rapinoe is my brother, and I am just like him!"

Brian played soccer, and as a result the twins dove into the sport too. "I worshipped him," Megan later said in an interview on ESPN. "He played left wing, so I played left wing. He wore No. 7; I wore No. 7. He got a bowl cut, so I did too."

Then when he was twelve, Brian's life took a dangerous turn. He began experimenting with drugs and quickly grew addicted. Megan and her family were filled with desperation as they watched Brian's health deteriorate. He was suspended from school for selling drugs when he was fifteen. He got on the wrong side of the law as well, and his infractions became increasingly serious. He was finally sent to prison, where he joined a gang in order to feed his addiction. His behavior was aggressive, and he spent years in solitary confinement for attacking other inmates. When he was released from prison, he again turned to negative behaviors to support his addiction, and it was not long until he was rearrested.

Despite the Rapinoe family's distress at Brian's troubled life, they tried to support him as best they could. Megan made sure to tell her brother that she had not given up on him. And that proved a great inspiration to Brian as he attempted to clean up and regain control of his life. Megan's success, personal bravery, and determination still fill him with pride. "I used to be her hero," he said. "Now she was mine."

In 2017, Brian finally decided that enough was enough, and Megan's example showed him that he had what it took to turn his life around. In his prison cell, Brian thought: "Look at all she's done with her life—look at what you've done with yours." He quit drugs, determined to start over. And not for a split second was there any doubt that his little sister would support him along the way.

TATTOOS

Megan Rapinoe's tattoos express the character and determination that have so inspired her brother and others. The tattoo on her left bicep reads "Nature ran her course" (meaning that she is who she was meant to be), and the one on her right wrist says "Trust yourself" in Arabic.

Megan Rapinoe's girlfriend, Sue Bird, and twin sister, Rachael Rapinoe (right), at the 2019 Women's World Cup final in Lyon, France

HER TWIN SISTER
RACHAEL

Megan and Rachael both became enthusiastic athletes as they grew older. They had many sports to choose from, but soccer came out on top. Megan spent most of her early youth soccer career playing on teams coached by her father. Later the sisters both decided to play club soccer with Elk Grove United, a team based just south of Sacramento. On Tuesdays, they piled into the family van, and their mother Denise drove them more than two hours to practice—an endurance test that would then be repeated on the weekend.

"They'd do their homework in the car, whatever they had to do," Denise Rapinoe recalled for ESPN in 2012. "We'd usually get home about 11, 11:30 at night. . . . We went through three vans during that time from junior high through high school. We just racked up the miles."

This proves just how close-knit the Rapinoe family was and how dedicated the parents were in supporting the twins' passion for soccer. And all that effort eventually paid paid off when both sisters earned athletic scholarships from the University of Portland.

Rachael Rapinoe was not far behind her sister when it came to soccer talent, but her path was also strewn with obstacles. At first, Rachael was a defender on their college team, the Portland Pilots, but she was moved forward after Megan suffered an injury. The forward role fit Rachael well, and she scored numerous goals and set up many more.

In 2006, Rachael played for the US women's national under-23 soccer team, but she experienced a severe injury a year later and was unable to play for a long time. She made an attempt to restart her career in 2010 by joining Stjarnan, in Iceland's top women's soccer league, where she scored two goals in five games. However, Rachael felt that she could not risk another serious injury and decided to take a break to rethink her path. She later announced her retirement from soccer and expressed an interest in pursuing a career in medicine. She got a master's degree in health studies in exercise form Portland State University in 2016. Rachael continues to be involved in soccer as a coach, and of course she supports her sister all the way.

THE REBIRTH OF WOMEN'S SOCCER

Women began playing soccer early on. Women's soccer became very popular in Europe in the years before and after World War I. On Boxing Day, 1920, there were 50,000 spectators at a women's soccer match in Liverpool, and some 10,000 to 15,000 more people were turned away from the stadium. In those days, women players were both admired and respected.

After this period, however, a calculated and consistent attempt was made to crush women's soccer by characterizing the sport as not "feminine." Women's professional soccer began to fade from the public eye and lay dormant for many years, even though many women still played recreationally.

Women's soccer finally gained popularity again in the 1960s, first in Europe and then in the United States. The first organized women's soccer league in the United States was the Craig Club Girls Soccer League, which consisted of four teams in St. Louis, Missouri, playing 15-game seasons in 1950 and 1951. In 1972, the US Congress passed a law called Title IX (later renamed the Patsy T. Mink Equal Opportunity in Education Act) to improve gender equality across the country. For example, it made equality mandatory for public educational institutions, including collegiate athletics. Title IX spurred the development of many women's sports, not least of them soccer. Soccer became popular with American women, although they still lacked professional opportunities. The US women's national team was established in 1973, and played its first international game on August 18, 1985, losing 0–1 to Italy.

Still, it would not be long until the US national team counted among the world's best. The team had great ambition, and powerful individual players soon emerged. The first FIFA Women's World Cup was held in China in 1991. The US took a solid victory—not surprising given the strength of the lineup. April Heinrichs served as captain of the team, which was composed of many soon-to-be legends, such as Michelle Akers, Joy Fawcett, Carla Overbeck, and Carin Jennings, as well as rising stars Mia Hamm, Julie Foudy, and Kristine Lilly.

That first World Cup victory failed to attract much attention, but this was not the case eight years later, when the US hosted the tournament. The magnificent US team lay waste to one opponent after another. They defeated two giants, Germany and Brazil, in the knockout stage, and then went on to beat China in a penalty shootout at the final, thereby taking a second world championship. This time the US women's victory was widely covered in the media, and women's soccer saw a significant rise in popularity nationwide as a result.

First match of the British Ladies' Football Club, March 1895

US player Brandi Chastain celebrates with her teammates after winning the 1999 Women's World Cup final against China at the Rose Bowl in Pasadena, California.

WHEN EVERYTHING CHANGED

"The '99 Women's World Cup came around at the perfect time for me. . . . And everything changed. . . . Nothing like this had existed. All of a sudden, there was a World Cup for women. . . . And people were going crazy, painting their faces and wrapping themselves in the flag. It was just this wave that nobody saw coming. . . . I think you probably had thousands of girls in the stadium that day who went home and grabbed a ball. . . . It was finally possible to dream that big."—Megan Rapinoe

THE NATIONAL TEAM COMES KNOCKING!

Megan Rapinoe gained attention as soon as she began playing with the Pilots, the University of Portland's soccer team. She was not quite a wunderkind but grew decidedly more confident over time, both at scoring and at setting up goals. Rapinoe eventually drew the interest of the USWNT, and made her international debut at age twenty-one, in a friendly game against Ireland on July 23, 2006. She scored her first two international goals on October 1, 2006, against Taiwan. However, Rapinoe's forward march was impeded by injuries, which prevented her from participating in both the 2007 World Cup and the 2008 Olympic Games in Beijing. Her first major tournament was the 2011 World Cup in Germany. By then Rapinoe had become part of the backbone of a young and highly talented squad, poised for the World Cup crown. At one point, Rapinoe scored a goal against Colombia and then ran to the corner flag and sang a few lines from the Bruce Springsteen song "Born in the USA," in honor of her brother Brian. She also made three assists. To the surprise of many, the US was defeated in the final by a tough Japanese team, and a major tournament trophy would have to wait—but not for long!

MEGAN'S SKILLS

Megan Rapinoe is one of the world's greatest soccer players. On the one hand she has incredible precision and cunning, in terms of both shooting and passing, and on the other she possesses a brilliant and unique ability to read the game. She usually plays left wing, breaking free and either dashing into the opponents' penalty box or delivering razor-sharp passes to her team's strikers. Rapinoe's many talents are on display whether she finds herself on the left or right wing or in any other position, and she often thunders midfield to burst open the defense or direct the flow of play to the flanks.

Rapinoe is a remarkably crafty and artful player, a soccer brainiac brimming with passion and finesse. Speed has never been her strong suit—particularly now that she is over thirty—but she is still agile enough to shake off defenders and take the shot.

It is also worth mentioning just how graceful and entertaining Rapinoe is to watch on the field. Her fans are never disappointed with her performances, and her teammates can always count on her to set up the perfect shot and make a calculated pass, all while wearing an encouraging smile.

Penn State player Lindsay Bach jerks Portland's Megan Rapinoe away from the ball during the 2005 NCAA Women's College Cup semifinal game on December 2, 2005, at Texas A&M's Ellis Field, College Station, Texas.

COMING OUT

It took Megan Rapinoe many years to realize she was gay. But when the realization finally sank in, she was entirely content with the fact. It helped that her sister Rachael also came out to her. In July 2012, before the US national team headed for the Olympics in London, Rapinoe was interviewed by *Out* magazine and openly announced her orientation. She said that she had not really been hiding anything; it was just that no one had ever asked her about it directly. "I think they were trying to be respectful and that it's my job to say, 'I'm gay.' Which I am. For the record: I am gay," Rapinoe shared. Rapinoe's openness was hugely important during a time when few athletes would publicly offer such information. The struggle for LGBTQ rights has figured heavily in Rapinoe's public persona ever since, and she proudly continues to fight for recognition and respect.

LUCKY

In August 2016, the *Bleacher Report* published an essay by Rapinoe called "Dear Megan," in which she gave life advice to her thirteen-year-old self. Some of the advice was about how to accept herself as a gay woman, and some of it could apply to anyone:

"I've been lucky enough to experience extraordinary successes. Never forget to be humble about these moments. You are no better than anyone. You do not deserve it more. Be appreciative. . . . When you are presented with opportunities to do amazing things and meet amazing people, embrace them. . . . Life will throw you some curveballs. . . . Be honest about how you approach failure. Don't just be critical. . . . Approach it honestly . . . and assess the areas where you have fallen short. Correct them and move on."

Megan Rapinoe is honored at the Los Angeles LGBT Center's 41st Anniversary Gala Vanguard Awards at Westin Bonaventure Hotel on November 10, 2012.

THE 2012 OLYMPICS

The US brought a highly motivated women's soccer team to the 2012 Summer Olympics in London. Getting the chance to compete at the Olympics is a special honor and achievement for athletes, and Rapinoe was determined to enjoy every moment of it. The US team had no lack of ambition—after all, they already had three Olympic golds under their belt. In the first game of the group stage, the US played against the rapidly rising French team, which took a 2–0 lead within 14 minutes. The US regained its stride, and a pounding header from Abby Wambach after Rapinoe's corner kick in the 19th minute brought down the deficit. Alex Morgan's resolute goal then evened things up in the 32nd minute. In the second half, it was the Americans' time to take control. Carli Lloyd scored a screamer after a beautiful cross by Rapinoe, and Morgan tapped in the fourth goal, following a long pass by Rapinoe and a cross from Tobin Heath.

The US went face-to-face with Colombia in the next game, and Rapinoe scored her first Olympic goal with an ingenious shot from outside the box. Rapinoe was unstoppable in this match. In the 77th minute, she slid a pass to Lloyd, who scored the winning goal in 3–0 victory.

The group stage concluded with a 1–0 win over North Korea.

In the quarterfinals, the US overcame New Zealand 2–0, first with a tap-in by Wambach after a fantastic assist by Morgan, and then Sydney Leroux wrapped it up just before the game ended.

STRAIGHT FROM A CORNER

The semifinal of the London Olympics between Canada and the US will long be remembered, for two reasons.

First, Canadian Christine Sinclair delivered an outstanding performance and managed to score a hat trick despite the stalwart American defense—yet even this was not enough to ensure victory.

Second, Rapinoe leveled the game 1–1 in the 56th minute with an incredible shot straight from the corner, without the ball even brushing up against another player. She is the very first player, and to this day the only one, male or female, to score this extremely rare type of goal at the Olympic Games.

In the 70th minute, Rapinoe once again equalized the score at 2–2 with a thundering blast from just outside the penalty box, the ball rebounding off the right post into the net. And Rapinoe would prove pivotal one more time in the game, but for another reason. One of her shots landed in the hands of a Canadian defender, and the US was awarded a penalty kick. Wambach took the shot and scored, making the score 3–3. Then, with only thirty seconds remaining of extra time, Morgan made the final goal, sealing a US victory in an overall breathtaking soccer game.

Alex Morgan gets a big hug from Megan Rapinoe after scoring against France during the first game of the group stage at the 2012 Olympic Games, at Hampden Park in Glasgow, Scotland, on July 25, 2012.

THE FINAL

The final was against Japan—a team that had defeated the US at the World Cup the year before. But this time the Americans dominated, beginning with an early goal from Lloyd in the 8th minute off an assist from Morgan.

Lloyd struck again in the 54th minute with a gorgeous solo run. Japan did manage to lower the deficit, but in the end it posed no threat to a US victory. Rapinoe could now boast of an Olympic gold medal, one of the most sought-after prizes for any athlete.

Megan Rapinoe celebrates after winning the Women's World Cup semifinal match between the US and Germany at Olympic Stadium on June 30, 2015, in Montréal, Canada.

In the first game of the group stage, Megan Rapinoe scored the opening goal against Australia with a deflected shot outside the box, after readily slipping past a defender, but the Australian team quickly evened the score. Christen Press brought the US back into the lead toward the end of the game, and Rapinoe then cemented the win with a spectacular goal after a solo run from midfield. Rapinoe was chosen best player of the game. The next matchup was a goalless draw against Sweden after a tightly contested battle. The final game of the group stage was against Nigeria, and veteran attacker Abby Wambach scored the only goal of the game with a fantastic shot after a sharp corner kick by Rapinoe. Later in the game, Rapinoe delivered a rising long pass from midfield to Alex Morgan, who broke free from the defense to dive in for the goal shot, but just barely missed.

THE 2015 WORLD CUP

The first game of the round of 16 against Colombia was eventful. Rapinoe picked up a yellow card and would therefore have to sit out the next match. Later, Morgan collected a magnificent pass from Rapinoe and sped into the defense only to be taken down by the Colombian goalkeeper. The referee waved the red card, sending the goalkeeper off and awarding a penalty kick to the US. Wambach took the shot for the team, but missed. A few botched chances later, Morgan finally swept home a goal for the US. Rapinoe was then taken down in the penalty area, and Carli Lloyd stepped up for the penalty shot, securely scoring her first goal of the game. The game ended 2–0, and the US was headed for the quarterfinals against China.

In that game, the US players were in a fierce attacking mode but managed only one goal when Lloyd netted the ball with a header in the second half.

Rapinoe returned to the left wing in the semifinal game against the stalwart German team, and this matchup was truly a meeting of powerhouses. Germany's star player Célia Šašić missed a penalty shot early in the second half, but Lloyd made the most of hers, scoring safely for the US following a foul on Morgan. Defender Kelley O'Hara finally wrapped up the game with a steady tap-in. Team USA secured a place in the finals—and made ready to face Japan. Now the US would get a chance to settle the score after the humiliating defeat at the hands of the Japanese national team in the 2011 World Cup.

Those who expected a suspenseful final were sorely disappointed. Lloyd drove in a powerful corner from Rapinoe three minutes into the game and another goal followed only two minutes later, with the Japanese thrown out of whack as a result. However, the Americans had just begun. Lauren Holiday netted a clean shot in the 14th minute, and Lloyd filled out her hat trick a couple of minutes later. She scored from midfield in a spectacular effort and one of the most brilliant goals in any World Cup final ever. Sixteen minutes into the game and the score was already 4–0, with the final outcome as good as decided. The Japanese got their act together and halved the US lead—with some help from Julie Johnston's own goal—but to no avail. Tobin Heath slid in the final goal for the US in an incredible win, 5–2.

2015 WORLD CUP FINAL
BC PLACE, VANCOUVER, CANADA
JULY 5, 2015

USA – JAPAN
5–2

LLOYD 3, LLOYD 5,   ŌGIMI/NAGASATO 27
HOLIDAY 14, LLOYD 16,   JOHNSTON/ERTZ (O.G.) 54
HEATH 54

SOLO
KRIEGER - JOHNSTON/ERTZ - SAUERBRUNN - KLINGENBERG
HEATH (WAMBACH 79) - HOLIDAY - BRIAN - RAPINOE (O'HARA 61)
MORGAN (RAMPONE 86) - LLOYD

Megan Rapinoe of Team USA hoists the 2015 World Cup trophy while celebrating the US victory over Japan in Vancouver, British Columbia, Canada.

WINNING MENTALITY

The 2015 World Cup victory gained nationwide attention in the US, and it was now clear to everyone that a new generation of soccer players had emerged who were fully on par with the stars from 1991 and 1999. After all of the team's hard work during the World Cup, they happily returned home to much praise and celebration. Given that professional women's soccer is less developed in the US than in other parts of the world, it was all the more impressive that the country had built such a dominant national team. Yet the fighting spirit and passion of the USWNT, along with their unwavering confidence and skills, had catapulted them to the highest summit, and they fully intended to stay on the top for a long time! Former president Barack Obama is one of many who fell for the team.

In December 2015, Megan Rapinoe tore the anterior ligament in her right knee while the US women's national team was training in Hawaii. The injury was severe, and even after surgery it was unclear whether she would be able to join her teammates at the 2016 Summer Olympics in Brazil. She would certainly not be playing a major part in the tournament. Coach Jill Ellis decided to bring her along nevertheless, because Rapinoe served an irreplaceable role in encouraging her companions and rallying positive team spirit. And that is exactly what Rapinoe did, even if she spent little time on the field itself. The US was disqualified in the semifinals following a penalty shootout against Sweden. The German team ended up taking the gold when they defeated the Swedes in the final.

Over the next few months, Rapinoe battled her injury but eventually prevailed and returned to action. However, she was still not back to her previous form and lacked agility. Ellis had faith in her and would pick Rapinoe for the lineup whenever she could. At the same time, Rapinoe became increasingly outspoken about social issues. In September 2016, she decided to kneel during the national anthem at a game between her own Reign FC and the Chicago Red Stars. When the game was over, she explained that it "was a little nod to Kaepernick and everything he's standing for right now." (The NFL quarterback Colin Kaepernick had knelt during the national anthem to protest police aggression and racism.)

Some maintained that Rapinoe's days as a top-tier soccer player were over—but they would turn out to be dead wrong.

In the summer of 2017, the US hosted the Tournament of Nations, a series of friendly games. The US lost the first game against Australia. In the next game, the US had fallen behind Brazil 2–3, and only about five minutes remained in the game. Rapinoe then received a gorgeous long pass from Christen Press, plowed into the penalty box, and took a shot from a tight squeeze. The ball went in after deflecting off the Brazilian goalkeeper. After two years of being goalless for the national team, Rapinoe was back in the game. It was a great booster for the team and Julie Ertz scored soon after. In the last game of the tournament, Rapinoe scored the opening goal in the 12th minute in an easy 3–0 victory over Japan. Again she took a pass from Press, elegantly dribbled past a Japanese defender, and drilled in a shot straight past the goalkeeper.

Megan Rapinoe had returned!

As the World Cup tournament in France drew closer, there was no question the she would be on the team. Coach Ellis counted on her. Yet few expected that Rapinoe would turn out to be the star of the tournament!

Crystal Dunn comforts the injured Megan Rapinoe during the 2019 Women's World Cup quarterfinal match between France and the US at Parc des Princes in Paris on June 28, 2019.

BATTLING INJURIES AND PREJUDICE

SUPPORTING RAPINOE'S ACTIVISM

"I totally understand where Megan is in terms of her willingness to talk about hard social issues. I respect that and I support that. I think those conversations should be had."

—Jill Ellis, USWNT coach, 2016

THE 2019 WORLD CUP

A RECORD IN THE FIRST GAME

The US team's first game was against Thailand, which also marked the World Cup debut of the Thai national team. Unfortunately for the Thai players, the game turned out to be a 13–0 thrashing. No other team has managed such a feat in World Cup history, either in the men's or the women's tournament. The US squad dominated the game so completely that they drew criticism for not doing what they could to downplay the humiliation of their opponent, given the uneven odds. Some said the US team took excessive pleasure in their goals and celebrated too loudly, even long after the outcome had become clear. Others said that the US team had in fact showed their opponents respect by playing against them full force from start to finish. The Thai team stood tall despite the crushing defeat and said they had no complaints. Alex Morgan excelled in the game and scored five goals. Megan Rapinoe scored in a counterattack after a slick cross from Mallory Pugh, who made three assists during the game.

2019 WORLD CUP GROUP GAME 1
STADE AUGUSTE-DELAUNE, REIMS, FRANCE
JUNE 11, 2019

USA – THAILAND
13–0

MORGAN 12, LAVELLE 20,
HORAN 32, MEWIS 50,
MORGAN 53, MEWIS 54,
LAVELLE 56, MORGAN 74,
RAPINOE 79, MORGAN 81,
PUGH 85, MORGAN 87, LLOYD 92+

NAEHER
O'HARA - DAHLKEMPER - ERTZ (PUGH 69) - DUNN
LAVELLE (PRESS 57) - MEWIS - HORAN
HEATH (LLOYD 57) - MORGAN - RAPINOE

US players take a moment to revel in scoring during the 2019 Women's World Cup Group F match between the US and Thailand.

THE GROUP STAGE

Coach Ellis decided to allow a few key players to rest before the last Group F game against the powerful Swedes. Megan Rapinoe was among them. Carli Lloyd led the frontline in a safe win over Chile, in which the midfield juggernaut Julie Ertz scored one of the three goals.

On the sidelines but not out of the game: Megan and her teammates cheer on Julie Ertz.

2019 WORLD CUP GROUP GAME 2
PARC DES PRINCES, PARIS, FRANCE
JUNE 16, 2019

USA – CHILE
3–0

LLOYD 11
ERTZ 26
LLOYD 35

NAEHER
KRIEGER - DAHLKEMPER (SONNETT 82) - SAUERBRUNN - DAVIDSON
BRIAN - ERTZ (MCDONALD 46) - HORAN (LONG 59)
PRESS - LLOYD - PUGH

2019 WORLD CUP GROUP GAME 3
STADE OCÉANE, LE HAVRE, FRANCE
JUNE 20, 2019

USA – SWEDEN
2–0

HORAN 3
ANDERSSON (OWN GOAL) 50

NAEHER
O'HARA - DAHLKEMPER - SAUERBRUNN - DUNN
MEWIS - LAVELLE (PRESS 63) - HORAN
HEATH - MORGAN (LLOYD 46) - RAPINOE (PUGH 83)

The match between the US and Sweden lacked passion overall, partly due to the fact that both teams had already secured a place in the knock-out stage. However, there was no question that two strong teams were facing each other, and both played with confidence. Lindsey Horan scored from Rapinoe's corner kick within three minutes of the start of the game. The second half saw a second US goal, this time coming off the foot of Tobin Heath, then deflecting off a Swedish defender for an own goal.

Megan Rapinoe in action during the 2019 Women's World Cup Group F match against Sweden on June 20, 2019, in Le Havre, France

THE ROUND OF SIXTEEN

The first game in the round of 16 started with a bang. Tobin Heath broke into Spain's penalty area but was taken down by a Spanish defender, leading to a penalty kick. Megan Rapinoe scored a goal by firing off a confident shot targeting the left. Only two minutes later, the Spanish team caught the US off guard and equalized. The going got tougher after that. The US repeatedly pushed forward only to be met by a tough and cunning defense, with Spain turning the tables a few times and launching into offense. Sam Mewis was taken down by a Spanish defender in the 75th minute, so Rapinoe stepped in and scored from the resulting penalty kick. It was an emphatic win over a strong opponent.

2019 WORLD CUP ROUND OF 16
STADE AUGUSTE-DELAUNE, REIMS, FRANCE
JUNE 24, 2019

USA – SPAIN
2–1

RAPINOE (PENALTY) 7   HERMOSO 9
RAPINOE (PENALTY) 75

NAEHER
O'HARA - DAHLKEMPER - SAUERBRUNN - DUNN
LAVELLE (HORAN 89) - ERTZ - MEWIS
HEATH - MORGAN (LLOYD 85) - RAPINOE (PRESS 97+)

THE PINK HAIR

"We Need To Talk About Megan's Pink Hair. [. . .] I was . . . AGAINST it. Phew!! That felt really good to say. My feeling was—you're going to the World Cup! . . . And hopefully, if all goes well, you're going to be memorialized in all of these pictures that will be around for . . . EVER! Plus, blonde hair is like—Your Signature Thing!! And Megan was just, like,

Nope. World Cup. Pink hair. I'm in. She got it colored the DAY before she left, without a care in the freaking world. I mean . . . if you were ever wondering what the Rapinoe Life-style was about . . . that's it, truly. (Also, I love it now.)"

—Sue Bird, Rapinoe's girlfriend

CONTROVERSY

Over the course of the 2019 World Cup tournament in France, Megan Rapinoe got mixed up in the ongoing media quarrels involving President Donald Trump and his political opponents. Rapinoe had decisively stated that she had no intention of accepting a possible invitation to the White House if the national team became world champions. She also attracted attention for refusing to sing the pregame national anthem. And, she criticized Fox News, a network that her parents (and Trump) often watch. A fired-up Trump attacked Rapinoe on Twitter. However, Rapinoe and her supporters shot back at the president without reserve. Rapinoe's opposition of what she perceived as the US administration's hateful attitude toward minority groups invoked Trump's rage.

TRUMP

"Women's soccer player, @mPinoe, just stated that she is 'Not going to go to the [. . .] White House if we win'. [. . .] I am a big fan of the American Team, and Women's Soccer, but Megan should WIN first before she TALKS! Finish the job!"

COACH ELLIS

"We all support Megan—she knows that. We know we have each other's backs in there. For our players there is only one purpose, one mission."

RAPINOE

"I stand by the comments that I made about not wanting to go to the White House with the exception of the expletive. My mom will be very upset about that. Considering how much time and effort and pride we take in the platform we have and using it for good and leaving the game in a better place, and hopefully the world in a better place, I don't think that I would want to go. . . . I'm not worried about destabilizing the dressing room. I think we have an incredibly strong dressing room. We're very open with each other."

SUE BIRD

"But then Megan, man. . . . I'll tell you what. You just cannot shake that girl. She's going to do her thing, at her own [. . .] speed, to her own [. . .] rhythm, and she's going to apologize to exactly NO ONE for it. So when all the Trump business started to go down . . . I mean—the fact that Megan just seemed completely unfazed? [. . .] It's not an act with her. [. . .] She's always been confident . . . but that doesn't mean she's always been immune. She's as sensitive as anyone—maybe more!! She's just figured out how to harness that sensitivity. And I think Megan's sensitivity is what drives her to fight for others."

THE QUARTER-FINALS

The Parc des Princes stadium in Paris was almost fully packed to its capacity of 47,000, when two of the tournament's most promising teams faced off in the 2019 World Cup quarterfinals. The backbone of France's lineup was formed by the legendary Lyon team, close to undefeated in Europe for years, and French fans couldn't wait to watch their favorite players snatch another major trophy.

Megan Rapinoe scored on a free kick in the 5th minute as she sent the ball hovering upfield from the left wing, through a throng of players, and into the net. This unexpected goal was a great start for Rapinoe and the US team. A majestic and intense battle ensued, and the fantastic French team took no prisoners in their quest for the equalizer. The US team switched to five in the back to better weather the attacks—which is a rare move. In the 65th minute, the US managed to turn the tide and surged into a fierce offensive. Tobin Heath sent a beautiful cross from the right toward Sam Mewis, but the ball was instead collected by a wide-open Rapinoe, who then sealed the deal with a calculated shot. The French team gave it all they had to stifle the US lead and finally managed to bring the score to 2–1 with a header by the amazing Wendie Renard, but that was as close as they would get. The French had been knocked out of the running. The home team was devastated but freely admitted that the merciless American behemoth was simply too tough to handle. And no one was more clinical than Megan Rapinoe, who became the first player in World Cup history to score a brace (two goals in a single match) in back-to-back games. She was widely cheered as she left the field just before the end of the game, once a solid victory was assured.

2019 WORLD CUP QUARTERFINALS
PARC DES PRINCES, PARIS, FRANCE
JULY 2, 2019

USA – FRANCE
2–1

RAPINOE 5   RENARD 81
RAPINOE 65

NAEHER
O'HARA - DAHLKEMPER - SAUERBRUNN - DUNN
LAVELLE (HORAN 63) - ERTZ - MEWIS (LLOYD 82)
HEATH - MORGAN - RAPINOE (PRESS 87)

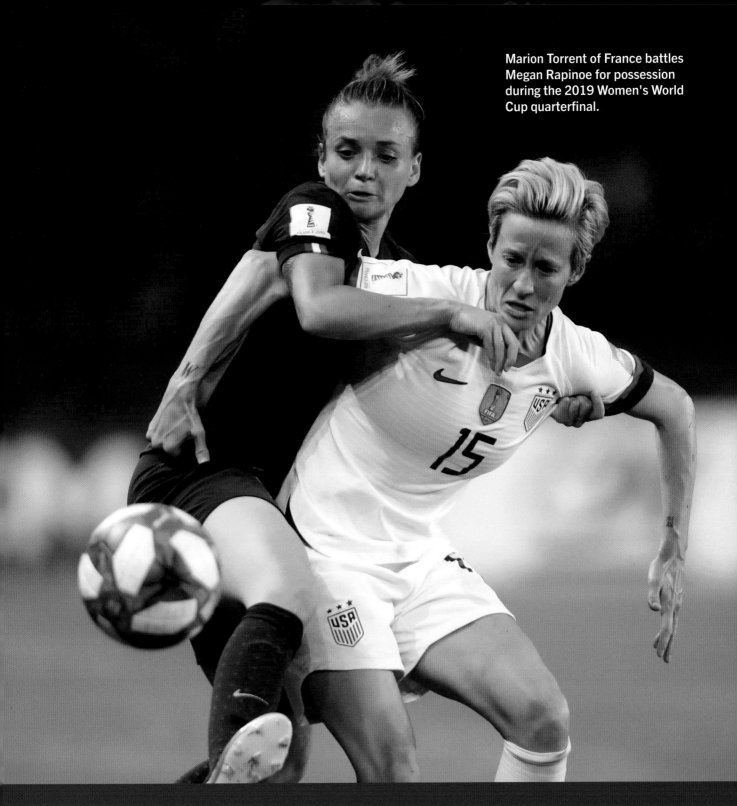

Marion Torrent of France battles Megan Rapinoe for possession during the 2019 Women's World Cup quarterfinal.

RAPINOE

"Our fans were amazing. They screamed their little hearts out, but they were no match for Les Bleus' fans. There was so much energy in the stadium tonight. France had a lot of the ball and energized their fans. That was such a big performance by our group. The focus defensively and the willingness and the discipline were tremendous, and we were ruthless in our chances. It was a game we'll never forget here in Paris."

THE SEMIFINALS

Due to an injury, Megan Rapinoe was not part of the starting lineup in the semifinal game against the outstanding English national team. Christen Press assumed a leading role in her place and scored a soaring header in the 10th minute. England equalized soon after, but Alex Morgan answered by scoring for the US with another beautiful header, and celebrated her goal by pretending to sip from a teacup. Morgan's goal turned out to be the final and therefore winning one. Toward the end of the game, goalkeeper Alyssa Naeher secured the US slot in the final by blocking a penalty kick in the 84th minute.

2019 WORLD CUP SEMIFINAL
PARC OLYMPIQUE LYONNAIS, LYON, FRANCE
JULY 7, 2019

USA – ENGLAND
2–1

PRESS 10   WHITE 19
MORGAN 31

NAEHER
O'HARA (KRIEGER 87) - DAHLKEMPER - SAUERBRUNN - DUNN
LAVELLE (MEWIS 65) - ERTZ - HORAN
HEATH (LLOYD 80) - MORGAN - PRESS

JILL ELLIS

"We're here for one thing, and that's to win the trophy. Everything we talk about and focus on is about that. When you are the premier team in the world, you're always going to have noise and external stuff. But we have a unique way of making sure that everything is about the game plan and preparation. The conversations I hear from the players are really about the game, which is exciting as a coach. They're professionals, that's the best way to sum it up."

Alex Morgan hugs Megan Rapinoe during the US team's semifinal match with England at the Parc Olympique Lyonnais.

RAPINOE

"When you're on the bench you need to be hyped for the team and give them energy and get those vibes out there. We dug deep again. This was the moment we displayed our depth. We had injuries, people were tired, and had little rest, and that's where the depth comes from. Everyone stepped up and they were ready for their moment."

THE FINAL GOAL

Megan Rapinoe scores the first goal with a penalty kick during the 2019 Women's World Cup final against the Netherlands.

2019 WORLD CUP FINAL
PARC OLYMPIQUE LYONNAIS, LYON, FRANCE
JULY 7, 2019

USA – NETHERLANDS
2–0

RAPINOE (PENALTY) 61
LAVELLE 69

NAEHER
O'HARA (KRIEGER 46) - DAHLKEMPER - SAUERBRUNN - DUNN
MEWIS - ERTZ - LAVELLE
HEATH (LLLOYD 87) - MORGAN - RAPINOE (PRESS 79)

WINNING RECORD
Team USA now holds the record for consecutive wins in Women's World Cup matches with 12, and for matches unbeaten with 17.

In the end, the US team managed a relatively confident victory over a challenging opponent, defeating the Netherlands in the 2019 World Cup final. The teams played to a roaring crowd of 57,900, among them King of the Netherlands Willem-Alexander and French President Emanuel Macron. The US president was nowhere to be seen, but a vast number of Americans did show up to loudly cheer on their beloved team. The US drove hard early on, but the Dutch put up a strong fight and had a number of scoring chances. The deadlock was finally broken when a defender fouled Alex Morgan in the Dutch penalty area. Megan Rapinoe stepped up for the penalty kick and netted the ball for her sixth goal of the tournament. When the promising young player Rose Lavelle leaped forward, ran the field solo, and scored only eight minutes later, Team USA felt sure that they would bag the win once again. The Dutch kept fighting, but a third American goal seemed more likely. When Rapinoe was taken out shortly before the game ended, the US crowd went wild: only moments away from the US's fourth World Cup title, they acknowledged Rapinoe's pivotal role in the achievement.

"This is crazy. This is absolutely insane. I'm such at a loss for words. I mean I'll find them, don't worry! But . . . ridiculous. First and foremost, my teammates. Just shout out to the teammates, everybody! This group is so resilient, is so tough, has such a sense of humor. . . . There's nothing that can faze this group. We're chillin', we got tea-sippin', we got celebrations. We have pink hair and purple hair, we have tattoos and dreadlocks. We got white girls and black girls and everything in between. Straight girls and gay girls. I couldn't be more proud to be a co-captain with Carli [Lloyd] and Alex [Morgan] of this team. It's my absolute honor to lead this team out on the field. There's no other place that I would rather be."—Megan Rapinoe

BRATION

WORLD

Team USA players gather with the trophy after winning the 2019 Women's World Cup final against the Netherlands at the Parc Olympique Lyonnais on July 7, 2019.

Golden Ball: Rapinoe was chosen as the tournament's best player and was awarded the Golden Ball. The runner-up was Lucy Bronze from England, with Rose Lavelle in third place.
Player of the Match: Rapinoe was selected the best player of the final against the Netherlands, and in the games against Spain and France.
Golden Boot: Rapinoe, Alex Morgan, and the English player Ellen White all scored six goals in the tournament, but Rapinoe did so in the shortest amount of time, and therefore won the Golden Boot as the top goal scorer.
Players Who Dared to Shine: The FIFA Technical Study Group released a list of ten key players of the tournament who "dared to shine," including Dunn, Ertz, Lavelle, and Rapinoe from Team USA.

THE STARTING LINEUP
IN FRANCE

Alyssa Naeher
Born 1988, Bridgeport, Connecticut
Club: Chicago Red Stars

Goalkeeper, height 5'9"
International games 57

Naeher was given no small task when she was tapped to replace the stalwart yet rather controversial goalkeeper Hope Solo in 2018. Naeher's powerful performance in France showed that she was well worth the trust. She, along with the other defenders, conceded only 3 goals in seven games, while their team scored 26 goals.

Kelley O'Hara
Born 1988, Fayetteville, Georgia
Club: Utah Royals

Left back, height 5'5"
International games 125, goals 2

O'Hara is a multitalented player who can adopt a host of positions on the field, forward being one of them. She now plays left back for the national team. O'Hara is at her best when dashing down the field at great speed.

Abby Dahlkemper
Born 1993, Lancaster, Pennsylvania
Club: North Carolina Courage

Center back, height 5'7"
International games 53

Dahlkemper was twenty-three years old when she played her first international game, and her achievements have been so outstanding that she and goalkeeper Naeher were the only players to start every single game of the World Cup in France. She is strong and steadfast, and rarely makes mistakes.

Becky Sauerbrunn
Born 1985, St. Louis, Missouri
Club: Utah Royals

Center back, height 5'7"
International games 171

For a big part of her career, Sauerbrunn stood in the shadow of Christie Pearce (Rampone), but has recently come into her own in major tournaments, where she now reigns as the queen of the American defense. She hardly ever slips up, and fiercely stops attacks while rarely leaving her position.

Crystal Dunn
Born 1992, New Hyde Park, New York
Club: North Carolina Courage

Right back, height 5'1"
International games 96, goals 24

On the surface, Dunn does not come across as a particularly robust defensive player, but make no mistake, she knows how to go on the attack and racks up an unusual number of goals for a defender.

49

Sam Mewis
Born 1992, Weymouth, Massachusetts
Club: North Carolina Courage

Midfielder, height 6'
International games 60, goals 14

Mewis was a revelation for those who were only loosely familiar with the national team. She is a strong but opportunistic midfielder with a keen eye for passes and assists.

Julie Ertz
Born 1992, Mesa, Arizona
Club: Chicago Red Stars

Midfielder, height 5'7"
International games 95, goals 19

Under her maiden name of Julie Johnston, she was one of the backbones of the US defense at the 2015 World Cup. Ertz dominated the center back like a military commander and set up countless attacks. She kept her stride in France, in a new position.

Rose Lavelle
Born 1995, Cincinnati, Ohio
Club: Washington Spirit

Midfielder, height 5'4"
International games 38, goals 10

If Mewis surprised soccer fans at the 2019 World Cup, Lavelle's performance was even more startling, particularly given how little she was known outside the US before the tournament. This gifted attacking midfielder is only headed upward.

Tobin Heath
Born 1988, Morristown, New Jersey
Club: Portland Thorns

Winger, height 5'6"
International games 162, goals 32

Heath has no intention of slowing down and
will not easily give up her position on the US
frontlines to her competitors. Passion, speed,
and sharp crosses are her biggest assets.

Alex Morgan
Born 1989, San Dimas, California
Club: Orlando Pride

Striker, height 5'7"
International games 169, goals 107

The careers of Morgan and Rapinoe
have coincided somewhat, and they
know each other well. Despite Morgan's trademark speed and unyielding
strength, she is also agile and tactical,
with a sharp eye for goals.

MEGAN RAPINOE
Born July 5, 1985, Redding, California
Club: Reign FC (Tacoma, Washington)

Winger, midfielder, height 5'5"
International games 160, goals 50

Ali Krieger
Born 1985
Defender
International
games 104,
goals 1

Lindsey Horan
Born 1994
Forward
International
games 78,
goals 12

Carli Lloyd
Born 1982
Forward
International
games 288,
goals 121

Christen Press
Born 1988
Forward
International
games 130,
goals 51

Mallory Pugh
Born 1998
Forward
International
games 62,
goals 18

Jill Ellis
Born 1966, Portsmouth, England
Coach

Ellis moved from England to the United States when she was fifteen years old. At that time she had never played any organized soccer. She played with a team in Williamsburg, Virginia, but quickly shifted her focus to coaching. She coached the UCLA team for a long time, but also served as coach for the national youth team and as an assistant coach for the national team. She became head coach when Pia Sundhage retired in 2014.

Ellis is meticulous and precise, and all her players are perfectly aware of what is expected of them. She usually manages to extract the very best from each player.

Allie Long and Megan Rapinoe during the ticker-tape parade for the USWNT along the Canyon of Heroes in New York on July 10, 2019

A TICKER-TAPE PARADE!

On July 10, 2019, the US women's national team received a warm welcome when they returned to the States. Mayor Bill de Blasio hosted the team in New York, and after a ticker-tape parade, the women were honored with the Key to the City. Rapinoe expressed her gratitude for the reception and delivered a now-famous speech that was shared around the world, appealing to all their fans to support and improve their own communities:

"We have to be better. We have to love more, hate less. We've got to listen more and talk less. . . . It's our responsibility to make this world a better place. . . . It's every single person's responsibility. There's been so much contention in these last years. I've been a victim of that; I've been a perpetrator of that. . . .But it's time to come together. . . . Be more, be better, be bigger than you've ever been before. If this team is any representation of what you can be when you do that, please take this as an example."

OFFICIALLY

Messi and Rapinoe in the limelight

On September 24, 2019, Rapinoe's outstanding performance in the World Cup was formally recognized with the most sought-after accolade for a soccer player: the Best FIFA Women's Player award. She became the fourth American woman to earn this trophy. Alex Morgan and English player Lucy Bronze were runners-up. No other than the legend Lionel Messi received the award in the men's category. Jill Ellis was chosen Best FIFA Women's Coach for her achievements with the national team, while Jürgen Klopp, with Liverpool, was selected Best Men's Coach.

THE BEST

WINNERS OF THE BEST FIFA WOMEN'S PLAYER AWARD

2001   MIA HAMM, USA
2002   MIA HAMM, USA
2003   BIRGIT PRINZ, GERMANY
2004   BIRGIT PRINZ, GERMANY
2005   BIRGIT PRINZ, GERMANY
2006   MARTA, BRAZIL
2007   MARTA, BRAZIL
2008   MARTA, BRAZIL
2009   MARTA, BRAZIL
2010   MARTA, BRAZIL
2011   HOMARE SAWA, JAPAN
2012   ABBY WAMBACH, USA
2013   NADINE ANGERER, GERMANY
2014   NADINE KESSLER, GERMANY
2015   CARLI LLOYD, USA
2016   CARLI LLOYD, USA
2017   LIEKE MARTENS, NETHERLANDS
2018   MARTA, BRAZIL
2019   MEGAN RAPINOE, USA

In her acceptance speech, Rapinoe thanked her partner, family, and friends back home in Redding, but also emphasized the solidarity of the American national team and the fighting spirit and unity that soccer can inspire:

"We have such an incredible opportunity, being professional players. We have so much success, financial and otherwise, we have incredible platforms. I ask everyone here . . . lend your platform to other people, lift other people up, share your success. We have a unique opportunity in football, different from any other sport in the world, to use this beautiful game to actually change the world for the better. . . . I hope you take that to heart and just do something, do anything; we have incredible power in this room."

MEGAN RAPINOE, CELEBRITY

Thanks to her amazing soccer career and outspoken personality, Megan Rapinoe is all over the media, from magazine covers to late-night TV shows. She has more than two million followers on Instagram and almost a million followers on Twitter. She is even writing two books of her own, which will be published in fall 2020—one for adults and one for kids.

Olympian Megan Rapinoe attends Samsung's Annual Hope for Children gala at the American Museum of Natural History in New York City on June 4, 2012.

Megan Rapinoe, Jimmy Kimmel, and Alex Morgan

Tennis star Billie Jean King and Megan Rapinoe at the Women in Sports Foundation's 40th Annual Salute to Women in Sports Awards Gala at Cipriani Wall Street in New York City on October 16, 2019

A ROLE MODEL—BUT ALWAYS HERSELF

"I don't really understand why there is such a resistance toward going all-in on women. It's pretty clear women in sport have not been treated with the same care and financing as men's sports have. No one is really arguing about that anymore."

—Megan Rapinoe on equal pay for women athletes in the *Washington Post*, May 24, 2019

"I want to be seen as a new offering of what a woman should look like—of what a woman really is. I think so often it's 'Oh, she's a really bossy woman' or 'She's a powerful woman' or 'She's this.' And it's like, 'No. That's just a woman.'"

—Megan Rapinoe, *Glamour* website, October 23, 2019

"THANK HEAVENS"

Let's not lionize Rapinoe. She is flawed, and she probably can point out her shortcomings faster than you can, especially on the field. [. . .] But she is an essential rebel: a defiant woman refusing to play by the anti-quated be-cute-and-courteous rules that make many men feel better about female athletes. She is a societal disrupter, born of a program of societal disruptors, and thank heavens that this individual decided to join forces with this team."

—Jerry Brewer, columnist, *Washington Post*, June 25, 2019

Alyssa Naeher, Megan Rapinoe, and Ali Krieger celebrate their victory after the 2019 Women's World Cup final against the Netherlands.